For Our Children's Children

REFLECTIONS
ON BEING
A GRANDPARENT

ঔঙ

Carole Kastigar

For Our Children's Children
Reflections on Being a Grandparent
by Carole Kastigar

Permission to reprint copyrighted material is gratefully acknowledged to the following: Excerpts from "Self Portrait," "Quilts," and "If You Want to See" from *Reach for the Moon,* copyright © 1994 by Samantha Abeel and Charles R. Murphy, Pfeifer-Hamilton Publishers, 210 W. Michigan Street, Duluth, MN 55802 (800-247-6789). "The Lemon Tree" copyright © 1995 by Jennifer Clement from *The Tree Is Older than You Are,* selected by Naomi Shihab Nye, Greenwillow Books, Simon and Schuster. "Of Grandsons" from *Cobwebs and Cockleburs,* copyright © 1995 by Millie Wolfe Fischer, Ananta Printing & Publishing. Quote from Suzanne Noelle Janes from *Coffee Matters,* published by Starbucks Coffee Company, January 1997.

Copyright © 1998 by Carole Kastigar

Published by ACTA Publications
               Assisting Christians To Act
               4848 N. Clark Street
               Chicago, IL 60640
               800-397-2282

All rights reserved. No part of this publication may be reproduced or transmitted in any form or by any means, electronic or mechanical, including photocopying and recording, or by any information storage and retrieval system, without permission from the publisher.

Library of Congress Catalog Number: 00-101208
ISBN: 0-87946-202-7
Year: 04 03 02 01 00
Printing 8 7 6 5 4 3 2
Printed in the United States of America

Dedicated to all Children
and
Grandchildren,
Grandmothers and
Grandfathers everywhere

Acknowledgments

I am deeply thankful for Jim's encouragement and support, and to the lovely parents of my grandchildren who are doing such a wonderful job: Joe, Elyce, Chris, Mike, and Julie. I also am grateful to my daughter, Lise, son-in-law, Lee, and my mother, who have enjoyed such a special and rich relationship. Many stories of friends as well as family have enriched this work. For this I am grateful to all with whom I have met and shared. Special thanks to the third grade class at Phalen Lake Elementary School in St. Paul, Minnesota, and teacher Kathleen Flannery Zannoni.

Deepest of all is gratitude for the gift of relationship to Grandchildren Troy, Tom, Adam, Hannah, Erik, Kirsten and Kirk.

Foreword

When my first grandchild was born, I was fortunate to have been at the hospital. When my son came out of the delivery room with the announcement that they had a son, I was unprepared for the awe I felt. It was as if suddenly there was a great space around me; I had, somehow, an expanded consciousness and had entered an awesome countryside. I felt like a great spanning bridge. My place in the universe was altered forever.

As we spent time together, I found myself in wonderful relationship with my grandchild. It seems there is a sudden and whole connection, not the attachment of a mother or the pride of a father, but another, new kind of deep connectedness that comes with the event and with the role: a grand fullness of mystery. There is something very spiritual about this role.

I find it in other grandparents, too. While it often is too sublime to wrap in words, I see it in our faces, I feel it in our relationships, I hear it within our words. It is very gentle, and it is very deep. Life takes on another meaning. Grandparents don't have to try hard to be loved by their grandchildren. For grandparents everything is already in place. We only have to "show up," just be there. However, it does take thoughtful care.

Being with grandchildren isn't the agonizing work that rearing one's children was. Although some grandparents are taking on that task when necessary, most of us don't have that responsibility. We hear and read a lot these days about how the lives of older people have changed. We are more active: living longer, moving more often, traveling, working, involving ourselves in more interests. No longer is the visit "over the meadow and through the woods to grandfather's farm" the norm.

Many live far away from grandchildren. Grandparents are living in cities and suburbs, in apartments and condos and homes, even in rented rooms and shelters. Many are working in new technologies; many are retired with a full volunteer's life. Some, more than we would like to think, are raising their grandchildren, too. Their stories are awesome and often heart-rending.

One thing we can count on in this time of change is that grandparents, their children and their grandchildren live as much a challenge as any relationship in this age. We need to hear from each other and to know that we're doing all right.

Lifelong Love

There are as many ways to grandparent as there are families, but one thing does not change. Children, all children, need love, real love—the kind that listens. We never stop being parents.

Our care with grandchildren is another way of caring for our child.

In the Grand Manner

We are called Grand Parent for no small reason. We find our child a parent, her child, our child but once removed. Every person is still a parent's child.

When my daughter and son-in-law added to this expanding universe, paradox arose. With every child, more love arrived, more heart room, more delight and more joy.

Another star in the universe, another stitch in the design of life.

Being Power

In his book, *Grandparents/Grandchildren*, Arthur Kornaber, M.D., writes that following parents, grandparents have more power in the emotional life of children than anyone else. That strikes me as awesome. That power isn't something we have a choice over; it is simply the way it is. How we exercise that power is up to us.

What is my choice?
>Stability
>Joy
>Love
>Acceptance
>Belonging

...all the ways I can think of to affirm their being in this world...a lot to think about and plan for.

A Grand Scheme

A question for me: What do I want to be for my grandchildren?

I ponder awhile. I do want to be love for them. Maybe unconditional love is easier for me than for their parents. I can simply be here, someone to count on, listen, encourage and not judge, to play, to delight in the child and to support the good that the child is learning. There are so many responsibilities and anxieties a parent has. I don't have to be responsible to form character, yet by providing these essentials I can do a great part in just that. If I do not, I actually neglect an important part of their formation.

*One never is free from living
a grand example.*

Stability

It is said that grandparents are the most stabilizing force in many families. That often includes a socializing influence as well.

A man recently released from jail said he never got in trouble while his grandmother was alive. He couldn't think of doing anything that would displease her; she was that important to him. I wondered if it would have made a difference in his life after her death if he had gained a faith that her spirit was still with him in another way: transformed.

Nothing ever completely disappears;
Grandma's energy is still around.

Belonging

There are as many different kinds of grandparents as there are parents. There are the cool and ordered ones who allow the children to enter their order and become that shape. There are grandparents who stop everything and simply give themselves over to being with the children. There are indoor people and outdoor people, spenders, cookers, activity-minded doers and slowed-down television watchers. There are talkers and strong silents, smilers and sober faces, flexible and rigid, jokers and serious folk, healthy and sick.

It doesn't matter, though. All grandparents are still a vital connection to roots and one's ancestors. We all learn to get along with a lot of different people who live very different styles.

Might as well start with each other.

Building Independence

Children find it hard to accept advice from parents because they are impatient to be independent of them. Grandparents are important because it's easier to listen to their experience, wisdom and advice.

We all need wings to fly and roots to hold.

A Child's Gift

She calls him Bumpa and he feels special.
She'll follow him anywhere—
and his heart melts.

Nothing
can bring this distracted and busy man
to the here and now, to the present like
this perfectly faceted relationship
between grandfather and granddaughter.

Time
simply straightens itself out,
becomes all that it needs to be
when these hearts of old and young
meet.

(C.K.)

A Step Away

Grandpa, I miss you. Mom says you were a wonderful, happy, sweet and kindly man. She loved you, her dad, a great deal. I wish I had known you. You died when she was only a teenager and I don't have a "feel" for you. I only know that Grandma missed you a lot. She never mentioned anything, but I could feel her deep sadness when I sat on her lap. I was glad she was as comforted by my hugs and snuggles as I was nurtured by hers.

Love never dies. It lives on in our touch.

Being Sad

I had another Grandpa. He sat in his rocker by the radio, chewed tobacco and used a spittoon right there by his right foot. He never got up. I never saw him standing. He never joined in anything. He is a faint specter in my memory and I don't remember what he looked like. He missed a lot. He died when I was seventeen. I guess he was an alcoholic, to judge from the stories.

God grant me...

Grandpa-wer

I read that the average age of first-time drug use is thirteen. It could be a child can start as early as nine. Horrifying. Some seem to believe that grandparents have a lot of currency in a preventative role. Asking really strong questions of grandchildren is advised by the Partnership for a Drug Free America. They talk about "the power of a Grandpa." Keep them on the mark, they seem to say. It is not interfering to make sure they aren't led astray. We grandparents can often get away with questions that parents don't get straight answers to. Children are less likely to hedge with us.

"How come your grades fell?"

"Why are your eyes red?"

Oh, to have the skill to use love's power to avert a child's self-inflicted tragedy!

Laughing to Love

A bishop in Ireland says he believes humor to be one of God's greatest gifts. Humor can be a great bond-builder, educator and healer. It can help get over some rough spots like homesickness and loneliness, frustration, confusion and stress. Finding ways to bring humor into a grandparent-grandchild relationship is another enjoyable and creative endeavor.

It begins with chuckling over the mistakes I make. Ever find yourself putting the salt in the refrigerator? Or wearing two different-colored socks?

Laughter is an internal massage.

Knock Worst

There are dozens and dozens of books for children on our shelves here at home, but one of the very favorites is the old book with the knock-knock jokes and colorful pictures that move and tickle our funny bones.

Knock, knock.
Who's there?
Juan.
Juan who?
Wanna come over and play with me?
Ho ho ho!

Do you remember? Which is your favorite? Sometimes it's fun to make them up together or to collect them.

Of course you have to be sure to laugh very hard at the punch line!

Grand Memory

What do you remember about Grandmother? I remember sitting on her lap. It seemed there was nothing else for her to do but hold me on her lap in the rocker. She'd sing that funny little tune. Non-tune, really. I felt so perfectly connected and relaxed. I felt so accepted...no demands. Everything was all right just then. I don't remember much that she ever actually said to me or told me. I just felt her profound depth and caring protection through my skin.

I have held my grandchildren in my Grandma's rocker and hoped the depth and caring of generations passed through my skin to theirs.

Healing Bruises

Stability can be a tremendous comfort when things get rocky at home. Modern life carries many tensions; living with the same people day after day creates many more. The demand on time and performance leaves one breathless.

A little "boring" respite at Gram and Gramps' place can be a retreat for a bruised spirit. It is often a tremendous challenge to create quiet moments in this frenetic pace of the daily American life.

We need these moments so badly.

At Grandmother's Table

The bread hot and succulent
The yeast fragrancing the kitchen.
Memories of her strong, floury arms
Transforming matter.
Bone-memory; years of observing
   her mother
and her own practice of the crafts
Until preparing food has become an art
   and a sacrament of love.

(C.K.)

Sacred Space

The strongest association grandchildren have with their grandmothers is food. They remember the smell of the kitchen, the gathering at the table. There is something very primal about grandmothers' tables. Lots of stories get told there, and lots of hungers are fed there. It is one of the most sacred places in the home.

One grandma used to give a sharp reminder to anyone who would try to sit or lean their body against that table. "Stop that, we eat there!"

In every grandparent's home a meal can be a sacred event.

Sacred Tradition

In all cultures, every tradition's sacred event includes the celebration around food. Grandparents carry the tradition. My yoga teacher told me that in the tradition in India, meal preparation is a prayerful time. When the woman enters the kitchen, she concentrates on the people for whom she prepares food. It becomes a meditation. If anyone enters the sacred space and upsets this meditation, the food is considered contaminated and she must begin again with fresh food.

Father Greg Schaeffer from Sanlucas Toleman said that in the villages of Guatemala, preparing food for eating is the holiest act, for which women are held in highest esteem.

To prepare food is to call upon angels.

Cooking Lessons

Here in America it is a well-known fact that children enter the kitchen action very early. Kirk, at one year of age, already knows where to find all the pots and pans in Grammy and Bumpa's house. When meal time approaches, percussion begins! An improvisation of "The Kitchen Symphony" is being composed at that meal preparation.

Kirk "cooks!"

Talent blooms under bemused acceptance.

The Journey and Food

Eating is a most basic act of life. Without the proper growing, harvesting, preservation, preparation and serving of food, human life on the planet does not flourish or even exist. Without proper nourishment, there is no health, no ability to move, think, work, love and create. Food has always been recognized in every culture, and in every religion, as the spiritual symbol of the gift of life.

In the Eucharist, food is considered sacramental and metaphorical. Without food we cannot be food for one another.

This culture's subtle but complete success in convincing us that working in the preparation of food is inferior and oppressive is in itself an unholy act.

Ritual of Love

Different families have different traditions. In Steve's mixed home it was Grandmother who remembered the Sabbath and helped his father remember to pray and remind Steve that he was Jewish, too. It was the time each week when his father would gently and tenderly lay his hand on Steve's head during Shabbat prayer to let him know of his love.

This is one of Steve's most positive memories of his father.

Traditions keep the love in.

Food for the Journey

Religion is a way to recognize and live out spirituality. As children, both my husband and I were reared in a religion that encouraged us to recognize God's Spirit in every relationship we encountered. It encouraged the practice of love by offering a listening and sharing heart to everyone we met.

Our religion ritualizes that loving reality in its Sacred Stories (scripture) and Sacred Play (liturgy). We remember this Truth as together we gather around the table in community every Sunday. It has been profound in its simplicity. It has been life-changing in its practice. It has been healing in its authenticity. We deeply desire to pass this on through the ages.

Spiritual practice is part of our legacy to our grandchildren.

Story Time

The time came when my children's grandmother could not handle the big holiday dinners anymore. It was just too wearing. She was exhausted and we were frustrated but how she hated to give them up! Knowing it was time for me to take over that grandmother role, I talked to her at last. "What would I do?" she kept saying, feeling completely useless. "Tell the stories," I said. "Bring your album and tell all the family stories to the grandchildren and great-grandchildren." Quiet at last she pondered, and her eyes came to life. "I can do that!" And that's what she does and they love it.

Stories told well are always true.

Generations

We get out the family pictures and have fun putting them together and mixing them up: "Great-gram is Gram's mom and Mom is Gram's child and Gramma is Great-gramma's child..."

A parent is also always a child. There is only a larger opening that we make in this work of being parent and grandparent.

> *Grandchildren are our children*
> *but once removed.*

Family Story

One of the most important gifts of grandparents is telling stories of the family: stories that have been meaningful and delightful to us, that bring out the positive experiences of our family's life. Children love to hear stories of their parents when they were children, love to hear how we loved our children.

*Stories identify us, inspire us,
ground us, guide us.*

Story Circle

I asked the healing circle, "What is your favorite childhood story?" Out of nine participants, seven said it was a story that their grandparents told them. It wasn't the story that they remembered as much as the fact that their grandparent told it. "I'd ask her to tell it again and again. I don't know why. She just sounded so fierce telling about that poor man who came to the door. I loved just hearing her tell it."

Grandparent's stories sink in and heal, inspire and encourage.

Making Story

Dearest Child, I love telling you stories about when I was young and small, and I love telling you about when your mom or dad was my little one. You, too, have your story. Tell it to me so that you will know who you are, unique and wonderful.

Our story identifies us, holds us, moves us.

Love Lines

Grandchildren, who bring magic
> Children once removed.

The scent of their memory
> Clings closer than perfume.

They are far away
> Yet are brought so close

by the wild tug of the heart.

(C.K.)

Good and Tired

The little ones are coming for a few days. I love it! I get so excited for the time with them; they are so dear.

My friend remembers how tired I get. He said he and his wife have prayed today that the children take long naps so that I have time to recover strength between care and play time. Thank you, Art and Kathy, and your "God of Naps."

Love is a wonderful way to wear out.

Faith into Compassion

My friends who are not grandparents yet but remember the exhaustion of being a parent, ask, "Where do you get the strength?"

Yes, I remember how tired I was in those days of being a full-time parent! The strength for extended stays comes from the same place it did when I was a young, widowed mother: my faith. It comes from seeing children, for my heart goes out to them. It comes from seeing parents struggle to be all and everything. It comes from memories and gratitude...

> "...for theirs is the kingdom of heaven..."
>
> (Matthew 5:3)

Transformed Energy

Certainly the energy and strength I have now can't match what I had 30 years ago. However, patience, vision, compassion, common sense, intelligence, wisdom, faith and the ability to choose the right priorities have increased. Not a bad trade. Energy went somewhere.

Call it transformation!

The alchemy of life: energy to wisdom.

Staying Connected

One of the biggest challenges is to keep connected to grandchildren we don't see very often. They can get beyond us so easily.

Sometimes it takes a lot of thought to find ways to stay in relationship. We try to make holiday celebrations and birthday rituals memorable but simple. Special visits to a certain restaurant for super fudge sundaes help.

Finding an interest to share together, like natural history, rock-collecting, bird-watching, gardening, music, theater, photography, cars, electronics, comedy and jokes, dance, sports...it all helps.

> *There's more than one way to be an active grandparent.*

Wonder Full

When my arms are full of child all regrets leave, lonely hours melt and bliss comes to bless this space. Wonder enters; time changes its quality. A deep joy seeps through my skin. Is there trust any deeper than this?

Even when they sleep I feel the house full of wonder.

Thank Full Times

When a daughter says, "Mom, I don't know how you did it," or, "I had such a wonderful childhood, I want to give the same to my children," or when a son says, "Thanks for giving me the values you did to hold onto in the rocky times," the breath comes a little easier, the heart is carried a little lighter, the tears are a little closer and the prayer is of deep thanksgiving.

Thanks to bring to the Table.

Quilt

In the sun, my grandmother would sit,
calico and gingham spread long,
like a river speckled in fall leaves,
over her skirt...
...she would rock, needle in hand.

"Life is a quilt made of many different faces,"
she used to say,
"a fabric
of different goals and dreams,
each with different colors,
different eyes,
different hands,
yet bound together by a single piece of thread."

(Samantha Abeel, Age 14)

Memories of Grace

What do people remember of their grandparents? Everyday gestures of kindness, life, generosity. Grandpa took me fishing. Grandma made spaghetti.

> "…There was the sharing of wisdom, opinions, experiences…exchange of feelings and ideas…the legacy of baking…I learned how to set a table, and to say grace before dinner. I learned this just by watching her and the activity of her kitchen. She was my generous and patient teacher…"
>
> (Suzanne Noelle Janes)

Every gesture of grace is a gift of presence.

Practicing Esteem

Eugene Bianchi in *Spirituality of Aging* says that practicing one of the arts—any of them—can inspire and ready us to be open to revelation. This encourages me to help grandchildren to practice a discipline in art.

Sue, a beautiful, gifted and professional musician teaches her grandson piano. My grandmother taught my mother to embroider. I bring out crayons, or we improvise songs and scenes. We dance. We make parades. To encourage a practice in children just may be crucial. It adds to their self-esteem.

Research tells us that children who do some artistic practice do much better in school.

Wide Love

Diane and Bill's home houses four generations from granddaughter, age 3½, to great-grandfather, age 97. The learning, the exchange, the richness and depth in this home are incalculable. Diane exercises Great-grampa, who is blind, daily. She, a singer-actress, also practices her own vocal exercises every day. Little Hailey practices and practices her songs until she learns each one completely. No one ever told her to do this. She sees and hears Grandma and just does it the same way.

Oh, the power of living example!

More Ways of Presence

A pleasure and an education: for a child to watch a grandparent performing a skill. It is a deep way for a child to learn. To see the expertise, the interest, the concentration, the pure joy of gardening, fishing, baking, playing piano, telling a story, making a basket, stitching a seam, wielding a hammer...what a rich and glorious gift to a child. Deliberate skill, with that sense of plenty of time; unhurried, relaxed, in full confidence of time's fullness. This is Grand Parenting!

One cannot just tell another how to perform a skill in words. A child senses the joy and the how-to-do things from observing the actions.

Connecting Conscience

One evening a group of friends gathered for dinner. They were theologically trained, socially conscious individuals, and conversation drifted to speculation on the core of moral conscience: "Where is it that persons really find the focus of moral training?" There was a small quiet pause in the conversation. Finally, a murmur seeped through the silence. "Ma... yep... Mom... Grandma! Yeah, that's where the real conscience is formed, from that connection..." A lively discussion followed on the ramifications of that conviction. Imagine it.

Focusing moral training may be unconscious but still active.

Listening to Love

Perhaps a grandparent's greatest gift to grandchildren is listening, really listening. The most important crossroads of my life were managed by the wonderful gift of being listened to and being heard, whether it was Auntie Flo, Mom, a friend, supervisor or priest. We can be a grandparent to any child in the village this way.

A grandmother confides in me: "From my granddaughter *I* learned how to listen. We took a long trip and it was wonderful. After a childhood of not being listened to and visiting the same on my children, I learned listening from this young woman, my granddaughter." How grateful she is!

Psychologists report that the complaint most often heard from teens is that they are not being listened to.

What are they saying?

To Better the Worse

I love to be with them in the good times and to help create lovely traditions and memories. I hope to be there in tragedy as well, to hold them, listen and comfort.

"Let nothing afright thee for all things are passing…"

(an old prayer)

Loving Letters

Our local newspaper prints letters from children now and then. When the subject was grandparents, there were more love letters from children on that subject than there had ever been before. They wrote with great warmth and affection about cuddling, telling wonderful stories, being praised, trading questions, gifts and, more than anything, about the appreciation for grandparents who just listened. They love to be listened to!

These grandparents in every way made them feel loved, loved, loved.

Of Grandsons

Barefoot boy with freckles on your nose,
and eyes that dance
with mischief perpetrated.
Catch a butterfly,
or warm your tiny toes
in sand that leaves
your footprints
oh so small,
to this your first adventure,
beyond the garden wall.

      (Millie Wolfe Fischer)

Seasonal Change

Nothing shines up a day like time with a grandchild. The *son* comes out and sonbeams flit around the house making it suddenly summer. It's never lonely in the house when these sunbeams are here.

The air is happy!

> *Having children in the home is a way of changing the weather.*

Walking Ritual

Just before it's time to go home, 3-year-old Adam finds Grandpa for their walk. Little ones find their rituals, for they are natural ritual makers. For all his own reasons, that walk is wholly important to that small lad. It matters not the hour, the season, the temperature. He brings his coat, tilts his head and queries, "Grandpa, we take our walk now?" And so they go, down to the corner and back, he chattering while Grandpa holds onto his hand.

…and their hands are full of treasure…

The Universal Bond

One year I was in Palm Springs over Thanksgiving. Grandchildren from all over the country flocked to visit their elders. They basked in the sun of each other's love and delight. You could see it in their faces and the thrust of their chests. They were gentle and patient with each other, and they were very deeply tethered.

It is the same all over, this bond between the very young and very old.

Contemplative Grandparenting

In the pressure of present culture, being with loving and patient grandparents may be the only time children feel allowed to be just children. There is such a pressure all around them to do, to succeed, to excel.

We can afford to take time for the great pleasure of simply contemplating the grandchildren.

Stepping Up

"Hi, Grammy, I went poopy in the potty today!" Oh, what sweetness to be invited into the news of life's mastered challenges. Graduation. To leave the security of a diaper, to move into another kind of vulnerability. To trust, at two, that all will be well even with change as mature as that. These are large leaps. And I am trusted to celebrate it. Yea!

No step is too small for celebration.

Love Ahead

Does support ever mean monetary contribution? It can be a help to a dream and, sometimes, to survival. Some older grandchildren are able to gain an education only with their grandparents' help with tuition, books, field study, transportation, housing or spending money. Some get help in setting up a small business, some in pursuing a difficult career. Susan was able to continue working as an actress only because of income from stock her grandparents bought in her name during her childhood. It didn't cost them much then. However, it contributed a lot to help Susan meet necessary expenses later.

Love pays off in many ways.

Lived Courage

Overcoming obstacles is our lived history. That's probably what originally inspired the "I walked a mile to school in every kind of weather" stories. It isn't so that we will be pitied or praised that we tell good obstacle-overcoming real-life stories, but to raise the hope and courage of the small ones. What a gifting presence that can be to our grandchildren!

Hope and courage raise esteem.

A Closing Circle

A grandchild brings both sets of grandparents into a closer relationship. I realize it is critical to the support of the parents and the well-being of the child that special efforts be made to get along, to love generously, to refrain from competition.

The time came when I had to share my children and grandchildren with other in-laws. Before all the logistics of staggering time was sorted out satisfactorily, I spent one lonely holiday when they were all gone somewhere else. To be sure I had some time with them, too, I began, from then on, a tradition of a Tree Trimming party. At least I was able to count on one yearly celebration!

Celebration brings our circle of experience together.

Just Keep On

When Erik was two years old, I found his name on an embroidered clothes tag. I thought it would be fun to sew it to his shirt pocket. He was pretty excited, but when I tried, the frail material kept fraying and pulling and coming apart. Finally I said, "I don't think this is going to work." "You can do it, Grammy, you can do it!" he urged. How could I let him down? I attacked the task with increased determination and a small prayer. You know what? I did it! We did it. I found that saying in an ad one day. "You can do it!" Now it's next to Erik's picture on my desk.

Some lessons of encouragement come in small surprising packages.

An Aching Love

Grand pain! We had earaches. We were there while our children had earaches, living the pain with them, feeling so helpless in waiting it out, even with medication and hugs. Now we watch again when their children have earaches. The pain is twice as bad. Wanting to take it away...the desire never fades, it only grows ever more strong.

As love deepens joy, so can it deepen pain.

Real Praise

Granddaughter of two sat on Grammy's lap as the celebrant gave the homily. She was drawing her musings on a little piece of paper with a yellow marker, very carefully. When she was finished she gave the marker back to Grammy and held the paper for awhile, gently, examining it, treasuring it. When the basket came around, she, without hesitation, dropped the drawing in. Offering: myself for you, Holy One. Amen. She followed my finger as we sang the sacred music. On the third verse she joined in the melody. Our prayer.

Praise was done that day.

Ongoing Creation

Anne teaches junior high. She says her grandaughter is her eighth grade "consultant." She needs her input to stay informed. Grandchildren will give us new eyes. God is doing something new and we can only understand it through these new eyes. What does it mean for us?

I am about to do a new thing; now it springs forth, do you not perceive it?

(Isaiah 43:19)

Grand Goodness

Their mother was driving the boys to Grammy's house and telling them to be good for Grandma. "Oh, we're always good for Grandma," they replied, puzzled that she would even bring it up. And they are.

What is this power that can draw desire to be good?

The Care in Child

Kirsten, two, calls everyone over sixty Grandma and Grandpa and she is sweet with all of them. She will take their hand to walk with them, slow her pace to match theirs and chatter. It is gratifying to see the softness settle on their faces, the carefulness in their attention.

Kirsten, are you an angel? An angel of peace? Could be.

Surprising and touching care from such a small child.

To Be The Best

I heard a story: A little boy and his Granny were in the garden one day. As they worked side by side, Granny asked her grandson what he was going to be when he grew up.

"Will you be a farmer?"
"Nope."
"A doctor then?"
"No."
"Salesman?"
"No."
"Lawyer?"
"Nope," he said. "I'm going to be a man, like my Grandpa."

> *Maturity, love and wisdom win over achievement.*

Materialistic Morass

Many parents are worried, very worried, about pressures working against their vision for children to be the kind of people they hope them to be: kind, merciful, just, responsible and caring. Parents who know the value of these ideals are way beyond the materialistic jungle of want for "riches and happily ever after." Encouragement in this realm takes creativity.

To live these values myself is the best way to help or encourage their teaching, ideal, vision.

If You Want to See

If you want to see the past,
look around you
for everything you do is
living out the legacy of those
who came before you...

...If you want to see the present,
look around you
for it is what you are building
for those who will come
after you...

...If you want to see the future,
look inside you
for it is here all the building
begins.

(Samantha Abeel, Age 14)

Burnished Golden Years

One set of our grandchildren has not only a maternal great-grandmother but paternal great-grandparents! It is a wonder anymore to see marriages last as long as Margaret and Mike's. They have been married for 70 years and are entirely devoted to and delighted in each other. Commitment and humor are the key. What a gift to their great-grandchildren to see them together and witness their love to one another!

A great gift for grandchildren is to be able to see their grandparents' love fill out the years…to learn what commitment and devotion looks like when burnished to a glow by time.

Shifting Gears

A new challenge: to parent our adult child who is now a parent. What does it mean? We've entered a new world and a relationship shifts, but does not end. It's much different from being a parent to a young child, even a single adult child, yet my being a parent is forever. An ongoing question is, what is helpful? What is unnecessary?

Hint: watch the grandchild.

Many Mansions

There are grandparents of a spiritual kind who have given up their own claim to personal family to be family to the lost. Sister Char is Grand Mother to hundreds of neglected, abused, hungry, lost and abandoned women and children who come to St. Joseph's Hope Community for shelter and guidance.

Char is a "singular parent," rather than a single parent in this case.

Staying Close

It can be difficult to feel close to a grandchild when we live far from each other. We can and do so love them, oh yes; that's not hard at all. But how can we bridge the pain of separation? I must keep up my involvement in the "village" through some means of communication, if not in proximity! Pictures, phone calls, videos of each other, e-mail...whatever helps. My California daughter and my mother have exchanged audio tapes for years.

Call me, my sweet ones! Send me your darling drawings! Let me know about your wonderings, your delights, your fears, your sorrows.

Together we can experience their gift and enrichment through our sharing.

Time Well Spent

Suddenly time has taken on a new dimension. My grandchildren will be here long after I am gone. What will they have to do to live safely and joyfully and prosperously? Things I do now will make a difference! With children out of the nest there is time I never had before. Spending some of this time in political effort ensuring freedoms and responsibilities, in religious effort ensuring joy and forgiveness, in social effort ensuring respect and equality...

...these will have longer reaching effects than twenty years in a retirement playground.

A Telling Story

What can I tell them about what is truly important in life? Wisdom, experience and awareness bring us to the appreciation of "essential" living. What is basically important? Joy, delight, trust, acceptance, curiosity, wonder in the mystery of life.

And the "telling" comes only in the example of living—the sharing in companionship.

A New Country

Friends of mine have taken on their new role as grandparents with uncommon verve in their third life stage. Their son, while working in another country, married there and returned here with a family. My friends invited the family to live with them. Their daughter-in-law came from a country where this arrangement is not uncommon but it is very different from the "norm" here. How challenging to take on such diversity! They all practice a new language, new life skills and new trials of patience. What a gift for those children to be surrounded by their love, beauty and generosity.

Security, acceptance and belonging from their very earliest years in a new country!

Overcoming Time

Some grandparents find themselves parenting their grandchildren, starting all over again. This is not new but apparently is becoming more prevalent. Often this must be done on an income much less than it would have been in their working years, and on energy much less than in physically strong years.

"Your kingdom come. Your will be done, on earth as it is in heaven…" Now.

True Wealth

We visited a sculpture gallery and found wisdom carved on Zimbabwe's Shona sculpture. It said: "The wealth of our village is measured by the happiness of our children." There's something to remember. Prosperity means more than money or material things. If we adopted that measure what would be the bottom line? The last time I checked, I think the wealth of our "village" here in the United States measured by dollars and cents.

All children are our grandchildren.

Fostering Resiliency

I like to read a lot, including material related to child care and child rearing. I see that much of the reading supports the finding that each child needs at least one relationship with an adult who is fully and unconditionally supportive. Many children who had very little to support them physically or emotionally in their immediate environment have been able to grow successfully because one adult believed in them and thought they were wonderful no matter what. That strikes me as a lot of power.

God loves you no matter what.

Color Me Bright

Too many children don't feel safe. In letters to our newspaper they recommend guards at school doors to check students for drugs and weapons and to have metal detectors at the doors. They are concerned about friends and classmates who go home to an empty house. There is sadness and frustration in their letters when they write about these things. Yet their joys are simple:

> "I would have all the teachers, staff, students and myself put all our money together and buy every child a 64-color crayon set so that their pictures would be bright and beautiful."
>
> (Gifty Akofio-Sowah, age 9, grade 4, Northrup Environmental School, quoted in *Minneapolis Star and Tribune*, Nov. 7, 1996)

There can be a 64-crayon set in every grandparent's house. Have a life of all 64 colors!

A Missing Link

When a mother never contacts, visits or asks about her mother-in-law who is, therefore, her children's grandmother (whom they love dearly) one wonders just what kind of grandmotherhood she is setting herself up for.

Kudos to their dad who does keep the children in the vital connection.

What Is the Measure?

Research found that the push for high achievement is causing symptoms of stress and a feeling of failure in fifth graders. Even in grandparents I see the result of this over valuing of a certain kind of achievement. Marge is the best homemaker, baker, grower, carer of the sick and the lost, seamstress and creative maker of art, cook, the best supporter, listener and all around lover of people...and she has been encouraged by her society to feel like she hasn't made it!

Not so! This is true success.

Writing Real

Grand mistake! I haven't seen a portrayal of a grandma on the television who isn't decrepit, eccentric or, on the other extreme, terribly chic. Maybe these unusual characters are more interesting to the writers, but they don't do much for informing the public or affirming the grace-filled lives of many elders and the fulfilling relationships they can have with grandkids and adult children.

Time for a wake up call.

Grand Challenge

How do grandparents spend time and attention when there are fourteen grandchildren? Maybe like the grandma who bought an old bus so she could take hers to all the places they loved to go!

There's always a way to keep the circle wide enough.

A Grand Pack

Grandmas carry colored markers and paper in their purses. Children can also find mints, gum, pocket games and small picture books. "I wish you were my gramma," says my friend. "What a Fun Sack you carry!" Thus grandchildren are not bored while waiting in lines, not wiggly in church and not misbehaved in the coffee shop; and I am never surprised in a pinch.

...but, there are jokes and stories about folks when the bag is empty.

Stewardship

I hope to teach my grandchildren to free their spirits to reverence, to find the love in every act of God's creation. Once, after the rain, all the worms lay naked upon the sidewalk. A little boy ran to step on them thinking somehow he was "cleaning up" something bad or dirty. A little reflection on how worms feed the robin and work the soil so seeds have a place to grow transformed the killing binge to a celebration of the life chain and the delightful cleverness of the Creator.

> *Walks can celebrate creation and teach profound respect.*

Lemon Tree

If you climb a lemon tree
feel the bark
under your knees and feet,
smell the white flowers,
rub the leaves
in your hands.
Remember,
the tree is older than you are
and you might find stories
in its branches.

               (Jennifer Clement,
      translated by Consuelo de Aerenlund)

The Grand Harvest

I learn that the quality of my dealings with creation, which includes human beings, is directly related to the One who gifts us with Life and creates all. This has been a greater and greater source of joy to me. I have taken up gardening lovely flowers and plants. Grandpa gardens delicious vegetables. It teaches us much about tending children and relationships; some good soil, some nutrition, a lot of attention and deep appreciation. Grandchildren are the crowning glory to blossom in the garden of life.

The sweet fruit is our relationship.
The bread of life.

Sometimes a Rock Garden

Does support ever mean challenge? Perhaps. It's very sticky to talk carefully and respectfully, fully listening on both sides, when there is something seriously bothering a grandparent about the behavior of a child/parent. Is anything more touchy? One would hope in the face of an unsafe practice, an adult child would listen. She or he may not. It may be perceived as an attack, depending on the approach and the personalities involved. There may be some real unresolved issues between these two adults. As in any relationship, one only hopes these things can be addressed with care and love immediately and not repressed, dismissed or skipped over in fear.

Removing the rocks may mean reforming them to support a blooming bed.

Prepare Their Way

"I can handle it, Mom, Dad!" Remember those early years when they had to find out for themselves that running headlong can cause stumbles? It still can and does.

"I can handle it." Now the stakes are so much higher.

Tensions can be so great in a concern for safety and care. It never was easy to let them make their own mistakes. It's even harder now. The risks are riskier. Their children are also going to experience the consequences.

*I can handle it...but, can they, your
children, my grandchildren?
Can they handle it?*

Boosting Sandy Soil

It is true we don't always get along smoothly. That's just real life. By this time, hopefully, we've gained a little wisdom on how to live with that. Continuity is something we can offer even when temperaments and personalities don't offer great compatibility. We were here before the grandchildren's parents were born. That is a profound fact for a young spirit and offers a great light to forming soul.

Grandparents may need to fertilize a sandy soil.

Games of Life

The children, ages one-and-a-half and two-and-a-half were having a wonderful time with Grampa at their "tea party." Grandpa made a part of the game sharing with others in the room, taking respectful and courteous manner with one another, and doing all this with such an enjoyable demeanor that neither of the children wanted to stop! Their mom reported later that they were absolutely respectful and mannerly at dinner that evening. "It is so good to have these values supported by you," she said with gratitude and relief.

Games and play have serious consequences.

Tree of Life

Being a grandparent is like being the trunk of the family tree. We carry nutrients from the soil and roots (our ancestors) to the branches and twigs (the families and children).

Trees leave fresh air.

Self Portrait

To show you who I am
I crawled inside a tree, became its roots,
    bark and leaves,
listened to its whispers in the wind.

(Samantha Abeel, Age 14)

Foundations

Today I heard of someone who doesn't believe in looking at one's history, mistakenly thinking it "keeps you from being forward-looking." How can you have a solid vision unless you have a firm foundation? Making a family tree, connecting branches, deepening roots, visiting places our elders come from all are very important. It gives us stability and identity, reality and truth. That is gift for grandchildren.

"Where do I come from?" is a question with a long answer.

A Firming Love

Kornaber's study reveals that it is vitally important to a child's emotional well-being that there be a real link to a grandparent.

When Hannah came home from the hospital we held a family welcoming and naming ritual. We read the story of Hannah from scripture. Her grandparents, her great-grandmother and her parents gave to her a blessing and a hope. Adam, too, though only two, entered into this solemn and touching ceremony.

Hannah was firmly founded.

Cultivating

The earlier natives of this continent have a saying: "We walk on the ashes of our ancestors." Treasure, that's what we are. Ancestors in the making.

May our ashes make sweet soil for the future blossoming generations.

Common Ground

Troy and Tom, then nine and seven, had never met their 95-year-old paternal great-grandfather who lived far away in another state. My husband, Joe, their grandfather, had died early in our marriage, when their dad was still a babe, so they did not know that side of their heritage very well.

We took a trip west and went to see Great-grandfather. They stood one on either side of his chair for about an hour, motionless and fascinated as he spoke of his life: his work, family, the first World War and his adventures and his role at bringing his son and me, their grandparents, together. Never before or since have I seen them stand still for anything for an hour!

Another grounding in identity.

༺༻

A Lesson of Life

We lived upstairs in Grandma's duplex when I was a child. My aunt and family lived with her, downstairs. I spent a good deal of time with Grandma. I remember little of what she said to me. I remember only her care and consideration of others. When someone in the neighborhood died, she would take my hand and say, *idzieme*, or "we go" in Polish. It was for us to help the grieving, to share the pain, to support, pray and contemplate the mystery of death. I learned sharing pain nurtures strength and love, compassion and sensitivity.

> *Contemplating death opened the wonder of life.*

For Resurrection

Too many people, to my way of thinking, discourage children from going to funerals. Please let my grandchildren come to my funeral, and great-grandchildren, too, if there be any. It is important that they see and mourn, have the memory and realize as they grow, that this, too, is part of life.

In death does glory of life awaken...

Vincent's Memory

Great-grandma. She helped me with words when I read a book. She gave me candy and treats. She let me stay with her. I loved her and she loved me. She read to me when I wanted her to. She gave me money and presents. She gave me pop and one morning when I woke up, my Great-grandpa called and said she was dead. I loved my Great-grandma not because she gave me presents but because she loved me.

(Vincent, 3rd grade)

The gift is in the giver.

Ances-Tree

When I die
Plant a tree.
When you see it
Think of me.
When you climb it
I will be
Holding you
In memory.

       (C.K.)

Leaving a Trust

Remarriage can be a great reawakening to everyone. When a grandparent marries again—after a full life and many mistakes—the saying "it's never too late to learn," or "to begin again" takes on new meaning and reality. New appreciation of the richness in trusting love, companionship and intimacy spills out light to the little ones. You can see it in their eyes. You can feel it in their trust.

Not all trusts are monetary.

Staying Vital

I am a veritable archive! I have so many stories and memories, links to the past and experience of what actions preceded the present conditions. I can love these children unconditionally, not judging but listening and believing in them no matter what. It is known that one of the biggest problems in society and among youngsters is a lack of adult friends. I certainly can do my part there!

What is my place in this vital connection?

Grand Gestures

Smallest children remember the things their grandparents give them. Older children remember the things their grandparents do with them. Oldest grandchildren remember the way grandparents listen to them. All of these activities that grandchildren remember are grand fun, all of them grandly simple. During spontaneous prayer in our church almost all children pray for grandparents and give thanks for them.

One grand gesture begets another.

Proximate Values

"Where's Grampa?" Every twenty minutes throughout her weekend visit she voices the question again. These little sweethearts do not understand about "previous commitments"; they only know that Grampa is not with them and they miss him. How the grandchildren love this lovely man who became an instant grandfather after taking up life with their grandmother. Somehow there does seem to be a void when he is not around.

An extended family need its extensions in proximity!

Gifts for Grandchildren

Easy time, no pressures. A chance to be still; time to dream and imagine, without judgment. Playing, smiling, hugging, leisure, emotional space. Education: sifting through experiences, seeking significance. Contemplating reactions, imaging new ways, listening. Companioning the soul. Loving their parents.

Love shall cast out fear.

Re-Careering

Have you noticed how many people in political office and professional activity say they retire so they can spend more time with their grandchildren? It's a trend!

That magic is at work again.

Love Crowned

What is this magic between my grandchild and me? We connect immediately and trust each other completely. This child sinks into my soul. I thank my children for this lovely gift. Maybe those years spent rearing children prepared this love field so fertile and fully in bloom.

*...For a tree sinking roots, and
a crown of blossoms ...*

"Grandchildren are the crown of the aged, and the glory of children is their parents."

(Proverbs 17:6)

A Grand Spirit

There are people who really think they don't want to be grandparents...yet. They don't want to interrupt their careers; they don't want to "baby-sit," they say.

And then the grand discovery! This is not about doing or not doing tasks. This is about relationship, and it turns out to be one of the most powerful relationships in the world. Suddenly the world changes. Of course we say "yes" to simple opportunities to be with these children.

*It becomes, if we are awake,
our spiritual practice.*

Defusing

I learn that creative challenges comes when there is friction in our relationship with adult children. It is important to work on the friction, yes, and it is also important to strengthen the relationship. Hold on to the good of each other and gently talk about the difficulties. It is so very sad when things get so bad that grandparents and grandchildren do not see each other. It is too precious and important to the children to have this love and companionship.

Buried friction takes on the power of land mines.

Forgiving Spirits

It may happen that even though we attempt to be good and caring parents and grandparents, we run in opposition to one another through different communication styles or different perceptions. Things are said and misheard; are skewed and misunderstood. In stressful moments, words are heard that were never said. Stress magnifies them, sometimes manufactures them.

How do we go on in the face of painful misunderstandings? Relationships must be maintained for the sake of these dear children. They need us. We need them.

We will continue to try, to continue to gently talk it through and to forgive.

Raising the Ante

Wait till you have children of your own! Remember those words? Now they have, so you worry about both generations. Does that part ever get easier? Not according to my mother who worries about three generations.

Grandparents can see far in their view back over the journey of life, and it can give them a far seeing distance forward. Sometimes the only way this perspective finds expression is in worry.

> *Prayer is better, I tell myself. Trust! Smile. Let go and let God.*

I Do Unto You

What does it mean to support our children when they are adults with their own children? First, I suppose it means that the grandparents remain consistent with the parents' standards and values toward their children as long as they are loving, caring, safe, affirming, accepting, respectful and courteous.

The golden rule, which comes through in just about every culture in one form or other, is still a good standard.

Life's Cream

What positive characteristics do children remember about grandparents? Well, they say,

Quietness, dignity,
Listening, laughing.
Taking time, savoring
Going slow, being calm
Marveling at life.

Planting, reaping,
Feeling, weeping,
Being strong.
Telling stories
Of creation's bliss.
And they say, most of all, they love me...

> *Interesting. All non-perishable and all non-purchasable.*

Incarnating

We were invited in the homily to "look up and see where God is in your life." See the places where "the Word is made Flesh." It is Christmas, and I see this child in my arms and I know the Word made human coming among us. Receive and nurture, for love is here and it will grow when accepted.

I look in the mirror and I also see God in my life. If not in this grandmother, why not?

God is everywhere. It was the first answer in my catechism.

Practicing a Grand Spirit

We are all born with a spiritual nature, and to develop it we practice, as we practice physically for the development of our bodies. Grandparenting is a spiritual practice. After all, we have a relationship with the Creator from our first moment. Therefore, every relationship is connected to that One. Everything I do in relationship becomes a practice in spirituality. When our spiritual practice has buffed our hearts to burnished gold, its light shines through the generations like laser beams.

Grandparenting is the most spiritually delightful practice I have ever encountered in the work of relationship.

"Bye, Grammy, I love you!"

The reward is so immediate.

Love's Care

Maybe the greatest gift we give is that we not only love our grandchildren but also love our children—their parents—fiercely, deeply, hopelessly, no matter what.

*That is what might be called
"the heart of the matter."*

Dear Child,

I hold gently the softness in your eyes, the trust in your hand.

I hold your heart.

In the End

"...and a little child shall lead them."
—*Isaiah 11:6*

"Lead, Kindly Light."

(John Cardinal Newman)